The Stuff Between the Stars

HOW VERA RUBIN DISCOVERED
MOST OF THE UNIVERSE

written by
Sandra Nickel

illustrated by
Aimée Sicuro

ABRAMS BOOKS FOR YOUNG READERS • NEW YORK

Vera always liked looking at the night sky. But when she was eleven,
she moved to a new house, with a bedroom so small the only place to look
was up through her window. As she lay in bed, a star slipped into sight, slowly
snuck across the pane, and disappeared.

Others followed.

The stars were stirring, and something bright stirred in Vera too.

Vera started studying maps of the night sky.

She read about the way stars fired their own glow, the way planets reflected the stars' bloom.

She built a telescope out of a lens and a long cardboard tube so she could reach farther into the heavens.

Every night, as the sun's light emptied from the sky, Vera switched off
her lamp to make her parents think she was asleep. She watched the
Big Dipper circle the North Star. She memorized the trails of shooting stars
so she could map their paths in the morning. And when Vera's eyelids grew
heavy, she dreamed not about what she had seen, but about what she had
not seen. She dreamed about the mysteries between the stars.

When Vera was seventeen, she went to college so she could learn more about the universe. She had already learned that young women weren't welcome in the "man's world" of astronomy. Her high school teacher had told her to stay away from science. One college suggested that painting would be a better choice.

Vera didn't want to paint. She wanted to observe. At Vassar College, she was
the only astronomy major in her class. She could reach into the heavens with
the school's long telescope whenever she wanted.

By the time Vera finished college,
she had fallen in love with Robert Rubin,
a mathematician. With their marriage, her life
took a new turn. Just as the moon orbits both the earth and sun,
Vera's life began to revolve around both her new family and the night sky.

As a baby grew inside her, Vera began studying a question that had left a trail through her mind. Was it possible that galaxies rotated around a center in the universe like the Big Dipper circled the North Star? She plotted galaxies on a globe, carefully measured how they moved, and then measured again. Just before her son was born, Vera concluded that her idea might just be right.

Vera drove through a snowstorm, thick as the Milky Way, to share her research at a gathering of America's most important senior astronomers.

The men were all clustered together like the bright bulge of a galaxy.

OUTLANDISH!

NO!

RIDICULOUS

They all seemed to
know each other.
Vera knew no one.

She stood before them and told them about the movement of galaxies.
One by one they stood up. They said her ideas were outlandish.
They said her conclusion was ridiculous.

Vera felt like the smallest, slowest star on the edge of their galaxy.
She asked herself, "Will I ever really be an astronomer?"

Vera didn't like the harsh words, pushing her away. So after she gave birth to a baby girl, she studied a new question quietly on her own—a question she thought would be a lot of fun. Were the starry galaxies scattered any which way across the universe? Or was there a pattern to where they spun?

As her husband and children slept, Vera stayed up with the moon and stars. She multiplied and divided and multiplied some more. At the end of several months, Vera had her answer. Galaxies were clumped together like dew drops on a spider's web.

It was a surprising discovery. It went against what everyone thought.
It was a discovery that earned her the title of doctor of astronomy.

This time, America's most important
astronomers didn't criticize Vera.
They ignored her.

She still felt like a faraway star on the edge of their universe.

As Vera's family grew with two more sons, Vera read everything she could about galaxies. She dreamed about observing them from high atop a mountain, like the senior astronomers.

She would watch as gravity, powerful at the galaxies' centers, spun nearby stars round and round. She would watch as gravity, weak at the outskirts, left stars to creep around their edges.

Vera began teaching astronomy at colleges and government offices in Washington, D.C. Little by little, other astronomers heard about Vera and her discoveries.

They wanted to talk to her about her "outlandish" and "ridiculous" ideas.

They wanted to see how galaxies clustered together like dew drops.

Through it all, Vera couldn't stop thinking about the mysteries she might find if she could observe from high on a mountain.

The Carnegie Institution had observatories in the California mountains. Vera decided it was time they hired their first woman. She walked inside, sat down, and announced, "I really want to have a job here."

Startled and not knowing what to say, the scientists invited her to lunch. As they ate, the director asked Vera to go to the blackboard and tell them about her work. He was so impressed, he gave her a job. At last, Vera would be able to see deep into the universe. She would be able to record images of what was there.

As senior astronomers crowded around other questions, Vera chose to study something no one else was looking at—the remote, slow-moving stars at the edges of the galaxies.

At Palomar Observatory in California, Vera's first discovery was that there was no women's room. She solved the problem quickly by taping a paper skirt to the stick man on the bathroom door.

And then, in Arizona, at the top of Kitt Peak, Vera got her first glimpse of the Andromeda Galaxy's outside spiral. Under the cool night sky, she watched the stars stir as a camera recorded the galaxy's spin.

When Vera developed the first images, she couldn't quite believe what she saw. The stars on the galaxy's edge weren't moving slowly like everyone thought they should. Even though they were far away from the galaxy's central pull of gravity, they were moving just as fast as the stars at the center.

When more and more images showed the same thing, an idea started turning in Vera's mind. Earlier astronomers had said that something mysterious might be at work in the universe—something that had its own gravity. Some called it "missing mass" because they couldn't locate it. Some called it "dark matter" because it didn't burn bright like stars or reflect like planets.

Dark matter, thought Vera. This mysterious stuff could fill the space between the stars. And then, like glitter caught in an invisible halo, all the stars would turn at the same pace. Dark matter might not burn bright like stars, but Vera could tell it was there by how it made the stars move.

When Vera told the senior astronomers what she had seen, some believed her. Most didn't want to. There was far more dark in the night sky than light. If Vera was right, it would mean they had been studying only a *fraction* of the universe.

Vera went back to the top of the mountains and took more images of galaxies in motion. The youngest wheeled like pinwheels, with their arms open wide. The oldest spun with their arms closed tight. Vera examined forty . . . sixty . . . two hundred. In every single one, the stars on the edges moved just as fast as those in the center.

The senior astronomers stopped shaking their heads. They finally admitted Vera was right. She had shown that the mysterious dark matter made up more than 80 percent of the matter in the universe.

Vera was no longer at the edge of astronomy.

She was at its very center.

Scientists crowded around the question, "What is dark matter?" Vera joked that it could be "cold planets, dead stars, bricks, or baseball bats." She wasn't bothered by not knowing. For her, the fun of astronomy was searching for new mysteries where no one else was looking—that and watching the stars from the top of a mountain . . . or from her bedroom window.

Each one of you can change the world,
for you are made of star stuff,
and you are connected to the universe.

—Vera Rubin

AUTHOR'S NOTE

Vera Rubin never forgot being told that her ideas were ridiculous and outlandish. Like a young galaxy, she spread her arms wide and drew in young scientists. She carefully listened to their thoughts, encouraged them to continue, and if they stumbled along the way, she caught them. Vera was especially encouraging to young women. An entire generation of female astronomers viewed her as their "guiding light."

From Vera's beginning at the Carnegie Institution, she worked with Kent Ford. Kent had invented a powerful new spectrograph. When he attached it to a telescope, it separated starlight into colors, like rain spreads sunlight into a rainbow. When faraway stars showed blue, it meant they were moving closer. When they showed red, it meant they were moving farther away. By keeping track of the changing colors with the spectrograph's camera, Vera was able tell how quickly stars spiraled in the sky. Kent Ford's spectrograph is on permanent display in the Explore the Universe exhibition at the National Air and Space Museum in Washington, D.C.

Vera's observations of the motions of galaxies, together with later observations by other astronomers, showed that galaxies do not, in fact, rotate around the universe in the same way stars spin around the center of a galaxy. Galaxies move away from each other as the universe expands. That was fine by Vera. She loved the way ideas change as we discover more and more about our universe.

To this day, we still do not know exactly what dark matter is. We know it's not made of the same stuff as normal atomic matter—the stuff we're made of. We know it has gravitational pull and that it doesn't produce light or reflect it. Other than that, we don't know much. When Vera died, she left the mystery of dark matter to "the adventurous scientists of the future."

TIMELINE OF VERA RUBIN'S LIFE

July 23, 1928 Born in Philadelphia, Pennsylvania

May 1948 Earned a bachelor of arts degree from Vassar College

June 1948 Married Robert Rubin, a mathematician and physicist

1951 Earned a master's degree from Cornell University

1954 Earned a PhD from Georgetown University, where she then taught for ten years

1965 Joined the Carnegie Institution

1965 Became the first woman to observe at the Palomar Observatory

1970 Published an article showing that stars at the edge of the Andromeda Galaxy were moving faster than expected

1980 Published an article proposing the existence of dark matter

1981 Elected to the National Academy of Sciences

1993 Awarded the National Medal of Science, the United States' highest scientific honor

1996 Awarded the Gold Medal of the Royal Astronomical Society, the first woman to receive it in 168 years

December 25, 2016 Died

2020 The National Science Foundation and the Department of Energy announced the Vera C. Rubin Observatory in Cerro Pachón, Chile

NOTES

Page 11 "Will I ever really be an astronomer?" Rubin, Vera. Interview by David DeVorkin, May 9, 1996.

Page 20 "I really want to have a job here." McKinnon, Mika. "How Colleagues Remember Astrophysics Pioneer Vera Rubin."

Page 33 ". . . cold planets, dead stars, bricks, or baseball bats." Rubin, Vera. *Bright Galaxies, Dark Matters*, 128.

Page 34 "Each one of you can change the world, for you are made of star stuff, and you are connected to the universe." Rubin, Vera. *Bright Galaxies*, 219.

Page 35 ". . . guiding light." Faber, Sandra. "Vera Rubin's Contributions to Astronomy."

Page 35 ". . . the adventurous scientists of the future." Rubin, Vera. *Bright Galaxies*, xiii.

SELECTED BIBLIOGRAPHY

Bartusiak, Marcia. "The Woman Who Spins the Stars." *Discover*, October 1990, 88–94.

Faber, Sandra. "Vera Rubin's Contributions to Astronomy." *Scientific American* blog, December 29, 2016. blogs.scientificamerican.com/guest-blog/vera-rubins-contributions-to-astronomy/.

McKinnon, Mika. "How Colleagues Remember Astrophysics Pioneer Vera Rubin." *Astronomy*, January 9, 2017. astronomy.com/news/2017/01/vera-rubin-remembered.

"Remembering Vera." Carnegie Science Department of Terrestrial Magnetism, n.d. dtm.carnegiescience.edu/remembering-vera.

Rubin, Vera. "Astronomer Vera Rubin—The Doyenne of Dark Matter." Interview by Josie Glausiusz. *Discover*, June 1, 2002. discovermagazine.com/the-sciences/astronomer-vera-rubinthe-doyenne-of-dark-matter.

Rubin, Vera. *Bright Galaxies, Dark Matters*. College Park: American Institute of Physics, 1997.

Rubin, Vera. "Vera Rubin." Interview by Alan Lightman, April 3, 1989. Niels Bohr Library & Archives, American Institute of Physics. aip.org/history-programs/niels-bohr-library/oral-histories/33963.

Rubin, Vera. "Vera Rubin—Session I." Interview by David DeVorkin, September 21, 1995. Niels Bohr Library & Archives, American Institute of Physics. aip.org/history-programs/niels-bohr-library/oral-histories/5920-1.

Rubin, Vera. "Vera Rubin—Session II." Interview by David DeVorkin, May 9, 1996. Niels Bohr Library & Archives, American Institute of Physics. aip.org/history-programs/niels-bohr-library/oral-histories/5920-2.

Thanks to Dr. Megan Donahue,
president of the American Astronomical Society
for the 2018–2020 term, for her guidance and support.

The artwork for this book was created with watercolor, ink, and charcoal pencil.

Cataloging-in-Publication Data has been applied for
and may be obtained from the Library of Congress.

ISBN 978-1-4197-3626-1

Text copyright © 2021 Sandra Nickel
Illustrations copyright © 2021 Aimée Sicuro
Book design by Heather Kelly

Printed and bound in China
10 9 8 7 6 5 4 3 2 1

Abrams Books for Young Readers are available at special discounts when
purchased in quantity for premiums and promotions as well as fundraising or
educational use. Special editions can also be created to specification. For details,
contact specialsales@abramsbooks.com or the address below.

ABRAMS The Art of Books
195 Broadway, New York, NY 10007
abramsbooks.com